THE ANABOLIC STEROID HANDBOOK

by Richard C. Daniels

KNOWLEDGE IS A POWERFUL TOOL

THE ANABOLIC STEROID HANDBOOK

Important Notice

This book has been written for information purposes only. The author is not a doctor and does not recommend or condone the use of steroids. This book is not intended as a guideline for use or a prescription of any kind.
Basically we do not assume any liability whatsoever for the application or use of the information in this book.

Written, published and edited by Richard C. Daniels.
First edition published Feb 2003

Contents

Drug Descriptions 6

Side Effects 33

Counterfeits 39

Orals and Injectables 41

How to Inject 43

Stacks and Cycles 46

Coming off Steroids 52

Eating to Grow 55

Training to Grow 60

Terminology 67

Closing Statement 74

Preface

This book is written in a very basic style, which is intended to make the information as easy to understand as possible. The level of information in the book will be most relevant to the beginner and intermediate steroid user. It is assumed that those who are at an advanced or professional level no longer need to glean their information from such 'text books' and are more than familiar with the chemicals and techniques needed to reach the peak of their chosen sport.

As you proceed through the chapters you will notice that I shall not attempt to blind you with science or give you a lesson in biochemistry, the information is laid out in a simple to read format. Most of the questions you may have will be answered in the coming pages. I will list steroids types, names and dosages and give example stacks. I will not recommend or prescribe, use the information as you see fit.

Polite Notice

At this point I will assume, by the very fact that you're reading this book, that you have already taken the decision to use steroids or intend to do so in the near future. One thing I would not assume however is that you're already doing everything within your power to both promote muscle growth and prepare yourself for the intended stack. This is where the polite notice kicks in:

Please do not be under the misapprehension that steroids are somehow a substitute for quality training and nutrition. I can't keep count of the times I've heard some fat lazy idiot tell me how …" well, yeah…I could be big to if I just took loads of steroids"…… PLEASE!! No you could not, I'll say it again, no you could not.

I'll spell this out for you, if you are not using a well tailored, resistance training program as well as following a high protein, high calorie, low fat diet with the correct nutritional supplementation then you have no business reading this book or using steroids. Put the book down, get down to the gym and speak to a staff member immediately.

For the rest of the masses who understand that weight training and nutrition are the building blocks and that steroids are the cement, I apologise. Now let's put the polite notice behind us and move on.

Drug Descriptions

This section is what's known as the 'meat' of the product, it's the chapter, which is usually put after six chapters of pre-amble. Not in this case. As I recall, the first thing I did when I got my first steroid book was to skim past the guff at the front and scour the drug listings at the back. Then, and only then, would I go back and read the pre-amble, the real information. So I'll get the listings out of the way first and then go on to explain the practical side of things later.

ALDACTONE (SPIRONOLACTONE)

Aldactone is a diuretic. It influences the body's hormone, aldosterone, which accelerates the excretion of potassium and reduces the excretion of sodium and water. Aldactone suppresses aldosterone, which in turn has the desired effect of excreting sodium and water whilst sparing potassium.

Aldactone is usually taken in the last week before a competition to gradually drain the water from the body as opposed to a sudden drain.

Dosages are usually 50mg tabs taken twice a day for 5-7 days.

Possible side effects are gynecomastia, low blood pressure, possible impotence, dizziness and muscle spasms.

ANADROL /ANAPOLON 50 (OXYMETHOLONE)

The daddy of them all, this stuff is potent, seriously. If you take 3 of these suckers a day for a month and don't grow then it's time to go home. As one steroid guru put it, "these things could put muscles on a tomato."

Of course every positive has a negative, Anadrol may be the most powerful steroid on the market but it is also one of the most harmful. The extremely dramatic gains in size, weight and strength are somewhat overshadowed by the fact that Anadrol is highly liver toxic. It is an extremely high androgen as well as an extremely high anabolic.

This is not a steroid for beginners; it is usually reserved for the already accomplished bodybuilder that has run out of other avenues.

Dosages are usually between 1-3 of the 50mg tabs per day for no longer than six weeks. This steroid is potent.

Side effects, amongst others, are: significantly Increased liver values, baldness, increase blood pressure, acne and nausea.

ANAVAR – SEE OXANDROLONE

ANDRIOL/ANDROXON (TESTOSTERONE UNDECONATE)

This steroid has received a variety of reports, varying from being hailed as "the athletes dream choice of steroid" to "being completely useless"

The basics are this; Andriol is an oral form of testosterone, but without the usual side effects. It bypasses the liver and is therefore not subject to destruction. It hardly aromatises (converts to estrogen), and does not affect the body's own hormone production. PERFECT, YES?

No, because of the short half-life of the 40mg capsules high dosages are needed. 6 – 10 capsules per day is the minimum needed to obtain satisfactory results, this may then tip the scales in favour of increased estrogen production and water retention. Not to mention increased cost. I have used Andriol in the past, for me it worked that is a personal opinion. The gains were minimal, slight muscular growth and slight strength increase. The gains were however quality ones which remained after discontinuing the product. Andriol stacks well with Primobolan and Deca.

Andriol dosages should be split out into 3-4 daily dosages after meals. The capsules are heat sensitive and will melt under extreme heat.

At higher dosages occasional side effects could be, acne, water retention and high blood pressure.

CLENBUTEROL/SPIROPENT

Not a steroid but an asthma medication. It is a beta-2-symphatomimetic. Basically Clenbuterol is not an anabolic but an anti-catabolic. (i.e. – it reduces the amount of muscle destroying messages in the body) Also Clenbuterol acts as a fat burner, specifically a type of fat known as 'brown fat' which is the fat used by the body as fuel. This is done by increasing the body's temperature to act as a furnace, a true fat burner.

Tablets usually come in 20mcg (0.02mg) packs of 30, 3 strips of 10. The dosages and regime depend on your primary use of Clenbuterol, muscle builder or fat burner. Muscle building regime is 80 – 120 mcg per day, starting with one tablet per day and adding a further tablet to the dosage each day until the desired peak dosage is reached. Maintain max dosage for 12 days and then alternate 2 days on, 2 days off for up to 4 weeks. Those concerned with fat burning would maintain the dosage day in day out for the duration of the course. At this point receptor sites are usually full and a 2-week break is needed before repeating the course.

CYTOMEL/T3 (LIOTHYRONINE SODIUM)

Cytomel is not a steroid but a thyroid hormone. This item is used to increase metabolism, which in turn burns fat and alleviates lethargy. It is an item which has many side effects and if misused can lead to serious long-term health problems.

Dosages must start slowly, build up and then taper slowly. Most athletes start with one 25mcg tablet and add an extra tablet every 3 days; dosages should be split through out the day. 4 tablets a day is max dosage, for no longer than six weeks. An off period of at least 2 months should be taken between courses to minimise health risks.

Side effects can include, palpitations, agitation, excessive perspiration, diarrhoea, psychic disorders and tremors.

DECA DURABOLIN (NANDROLONE DECONATE)

Where to begin? Deca…everybody's favourite. Renowned for promoting nitrogen retention (the primary reason for muscle growth) in the muscles, loading extra fluid on to the joints (which alleviate aches and pains) and being an extremely high anabolic with reasonably low androgenic effects. The result being good growth when used on it's own, excellent growth when used in a stack, an all round winner. It has little, if at all any, side effects on the liver and produces good strength gains with low water retention.

Deca, whilst being extremely popular, is also highly

counterfeited. Along with Dianabol it is probably the most counterfeited steroid on the market, some good, most bad. Avoid Multi vials (10cc etc). There used to be some great counterfeit flat packs a while back but dosages and quality seem to be sub standard these days.

Deca is a good basic steroid to start with and to add to just about any stack. As the famous Dan Duchaine said "if you can't grow on D'Bol and Deca you ain't gonna grow on anything, no matter how fancy it is." Very True, this steroid is ideal on it's own for the novice, stacks well for the intermediate and is a great addition even for the more advanced user. Make sure you do your research and get hold of a quality version, the counterfeits of this can be tricky to spot.

The average dose for Deca is between 200 –600mg per week. It usually comes in packs of 3 ampoules, 200mg in each. It stacks very well with Sustanon 250 and Dianabol.

Side effects are mostly mild, but with high dosage courses you will get nosebleeds, acne and headaches.

DIANABOL/ANABOL/PRONOBOL 5/NEROBOL/NAPOSIM (METHANDROSTENLONE/METHANDIENONE)

Dianabol, this is where it all began. Dianabol is a trade name, which is now no longer used but often referred to, for the substance Methandrostenlone. It is an oral steroid, which has built up many a famous physique. It promotes protein synthesis, gives a positive nitrogen balance, promotes calcium deposits in the bone and gives excellent gains in both size and strength.

This is another classic steroid, which has been used for many years by a variety of athletes. Dianabol is a fantastic steroid, if you can get a legit version. I have personally used it, over a 10-week course, stacked with Deca and Sustanon I gained over 24lbs, a little accompanying water and fat, but a lot of quality beef. Strength went through the roof. I took 8 weeks off and repeated again, obviously each time you repeat the stack, the gains diminish. I seem to recall a more reasonable figure of about 12 – 14lbs on the second go, still that's good going in anyone's book.

The Dianabol tablets fall in to the same counterfeiting problems as Deca, widely used, widely counterfeited. The best ones were the Pronabol-5 from India, not loose strips held together with an elastic band, but the little white 5mg tabs in strips of 10, pressed in silver foil with blue writing on, packed into pink and white cardboard packs of 100. Fantastic stuff if you can get it, as was most of the stuff from the P&B labs in Bombay. At the time of writing this book the easiest to get hold of was the Naposim in orange and white packets, same thing though, demand prompted the counterfeiters to jump into action. Back in the day the simple counterfeit of 'blue meth' 5mg tabs, in strips of 50 worked really well, but same old story here I'm afraid…. yup counterfeiters have churned out so much crap no-one knows what's in any of the stuff any more.

Dosages start at as little as 15mg (3 x 5mg tabs) per day and go up to 50mg (10 x 5mg) tabs per day. Dosages are split into 3 or 4 applications per day. Dianabol is liver toxic so dosages in excess of 50mg per day and courses longer than 8 weeks should be avoided. It stacks well with most steroids, especially Deca and Sustanon 250. Try and use Naposim or Pronabol 5, Anabol is a safe bet if you can find a reliable source.

Side effects include, High blood pressure, nosebleeds, acne and headaches. It does aromatise so Nolvadex (an anti-estrogen) is recommended.

EPHEDRINE

Club drug or Bodybuilding stimulant? Well both really. Ephedrine is an interesting compound, it acts as both a fat burners and a training stimulant. When taken on it's own it works well as a fat burner, through thermogenesis (increased body temperature) as well as promoting the release of the T4 hormone. Dosage on it's own would be 25mg three times per day. An interesting fact though is that by adding 200mg caffeine and 300mg aspirin to each dosage the fat burning effect can be doubled. This is the classic E.C.A. stack.

If you wish to use it as a training stimulant however, take 50mg approximately 1 hour before a workout. Ephedrine has a mild amphetamine effect on the central nervous system and gives a good training psyche as well as a mild but noticeable strength increase.

Side effects include, tremors, insomnia, rapid heartbeat, hot flushes, dizziness and lack of appetite. This compound should be avoided by anyone with a heart or thyroid condition.

EQUIPOISE/BOLDEBAL H/PACE (BOLDENONE UNDECYLENATE)

Thank goodness for vets! This is a veterinary steroid used for horses, dogs and cattle. Equipoise has a high anabolic with an average androgen effect. This steroid gives at best average gains, it is said to be very similar to Deca however Deca is reputed to do everything that Equipoise does, but better and cheaper.

Original vet' supplies are a bonus and would be preferred if you can't get hold of a reliable batch of Deca, this would be the only reason to choose Equipoise over Deca. Equipoise that comes from any other source is probably a fake; I saw a great copy of the Boldebal H version. It was in the correct green and white packaging with imprinted expiry dates, however on closer inspection I noted the label was not 100%. It would seem a standard 10cc bottle with god knows what as the content was being sold as "whatever label we choose to put on it" Same fake, 10 different labelling kits! Stick with a quality Deca.

Dosages are usually in the region of 150-400mg per week, if you're using the 50mg per 2ml version your in for quite a few jabs per week or massive dosage weekly injections, ouch.

Side effects are very similar to Deca, although it allegedly does not aromatise quite as much.

FINAJECT (TRENBOLONE ACETATE)

I'll be brief on this one, this compound has not been legitimately manufactured for over 15 years, if you get some, it's probably a fake. Good or bad fake…I couldn't tell you. Today's good fake is tomorrow's rubbish. A generic South African version was available for a while; try for this version if any.

The original was a powerful tool if used correctly, high androgen, high anabolic with terrific strength gains but low water retention, therefore not much increase in body weight. It was useful for strength athletes not wanting to go up in bodyweight, and gave body builders solid gains and was a great addition to a stack. The solid gains and strength increases are overshadowed somewhat by the considerable number of side effects.

These would include, kidney damage, headaches,

gynecomastia, acne, high blood pressure and severe aggression.

Dosages would sally be in the region of 1 x 30mg shot every other day, a high dosage would be 1 – 2 30mg shot every day. At this point gains would be outrageous, but dangerous.

HALOTESTEN (FLUXYMESTERONE)

Halotesten is a high androgen compound, which is both powerful and toxic. If you need aggression and strength gains you might get some use from it, but there are many other drugs that do this more effectively and safely. As a pre-contest drug it will add density to the physique. It is however one of the most liver toxic steroids around.
If you must use it, take no more than 20-30 mg per day for 4-6 weeks.

Side effect, yes, lots of them. Mainly liver toxicity but you can count an all the usual suspects.

H.C.G. (HUMAN CHORIONIC GONADOTROPIN)

This drug is manufactured from the urine of pregnant women, nice. It comes in a dried crystal format; there will always be 2 vials per dose. One vial has the HCG the other has a quantity off sterilised water; the 2 are mixed together to form the HCG solution.

When on a course of steroids one of the known side effects is reduced production of testosterone by the body, as you are adding it artificially by taking steroids. It is considered a wise precaution to take a shot of HCG firstly mid-course and then secondly at the end of the course. This ensures that a) your own testosterone producing glands do not stay dormant for too long and b) to help kick start testosterone production at the end of a course, which will in turn prevent a post stack 'crash'.

Whilst it is not wise to leave your body's testosterone production shut down for too long, it is also unwise to artificially stimulate it for too long. Limit the use of HCG to a couple of weeks at a time with long breaks in between. Other wise the body may become reliant on it for testosterone production.

As it increases the body's production of testosterone the side affects are very similar, if not the same, to testosterone itself. Headaches, oily skin, increased sex drive and water retention.

Dosages would be in the range of, a 1000iu shot mid course and another two 2000iu shots post stack, the first 7 days after the last use of steroids and the second 7 days later.

HUMAN GROWTH HORMONE (SOMATROPIN)

This topic needs to be addressed although the item itself should really only be used by top-level athletes. There doesn't seem to be any doubt that as part of steroid cycle, and with the correct use of insulin, growth hormone works tremendously well. There is however some controversy surrounding the theory that it works well on it's own. Apparently it does not. There is also no doubt that it is very expensive, if you get offered cheap GH it's probably a fake. I even heard rumours that HCG was being re-packaged and sold as GH. Of course introduce a stack of HCG into your cycle and things are bound to go BOOM! However this is a) the wrong way to use HCG and b) a very expensive way to use HCG. Apparently you can test the GH with a pregnancy testing kit to see if it is really HCG, as

HCG is manufactured from the urine of pregnant women. Not sure if that is a sure fire technique or not.

The other topic for discussion is side effects. Excessive use over prolonged periods can cause some nasty side effects. These would typically include, diabetes, enlarged heart, enlarged kidneys, thyroid insufficiency and elongated jawbone. Note how most athletes who use excessive amounts of GH also have protruding bellies, taking on a 'pregnant' appearance. How this detracts from the original and classic V-Taper of the past. GH has the potential to create some monster physiques, like wise it can destroy classic aesthetic lines and symmetry.

If you do intend to use GH then the choice product is apparently Humatrope by Lilly, the dosages seem to range from between 4 – 16 iu per day. The use of a high androgen steroid/steroids and HCG goes without saying. The product has a very short half-life so the dosages should be split into 4 daily subcutaneous injections. Once the product has been mixed together it must be used immediately or stored in a fridge for no longer than 24 hrs. Your daily meals should be split into 6-8 portions so that you eat every 2-3 hours, this will cause a continuous release of insulin from the body.

If you are using GH during a diet phase you will need to add an external source of insulin and thyroid medication.
This is where things get complicated, very. Too much insulin and at best you'll end up being fat at worst you'll die, too little and you'll just cancel out the effects of the GH.
Play with insulin and Thyroid medication and you could line yourself up for a whole host of health problems. The trouble being this, every person's tolerances and needs are different and specific to their drug use, training, body type and diet.
Get it bang on the button and you gonna get big, get it wrong and you gonna regret it. Either way it'll cost you a packet.
If you must play with insulin and thyroid medication make

sure you can afford it and make sure you know what you're doing.

LASIX (FUROSEMIDE)

Lasix is a diuretic, a powerful one. It's given many a champion the first place trophy and it'd robbed many a bodybuilder of life. When it is used, as well as squeezing out every last ounce of water from the athletes body it will also make muscles look flat. This can be compensated by an i.v. addition of glucose solution or the use of potassium chloride tablets. Introducing too much Potassium however will result in cardiac arrest. Most body builders take half of a 40mg tablet every few hours leading up to the contest depending how much water they have left and how far they are willing to push it. This is a most powerful diuretic, there is no doubt it will shift the water you are holding pre-contest, it is also a tricky drug to use correctly. Get it right and you'll be full, pumped and dry as a bone. Get it wrong and at best you'll look flat, at worst you'll be dead.

LAURABOLIN (NANDROLONE LAURATE)

This is not a particularly special steroid, very similar to Deca although it is shown to make you hold mare water and it is slightly longer lasting. Also it only comes in strengths of 50 mg per ml so lots of injections or large doses are required. It is actually another veterinary product, again, same as Equipoise applies. If you can get a quality Deca go with it, if not then try Laurabolin. There aren't to many fakes around but the multi use vials (50cc etc) are always subject to abuse by the counterfeiters.

Dosages and side effects are the same as Deca.

L-THYROXINE (LEVOTHYROXINE SODIUM)

This is a synthetic version of the naturally occurring chemical L-T4, the weaker version of L-T3. It is a thyroid medication that is used to burn off fat pre-contest. In order to maintain muscle mass whilst using this product, steroids must be used. Otherwise carbs are burned along with the fat and muscle shrinkage will occur. Cytomel and Triacana are now the preferred choice over L-Thyroxin.

Most use 200 – 400 mcg per day. It is very important to start with a small dosage and build up, do not stay on it for long and then taper down slowly and evenly.

Misuse and/or incorrect dosage/taper of this drug will lead to long term thyroid problems as well as unpleasant side effects such as heart palpitations, diarrhoea, sweating, trembling and insomnia.

MASTERON (DROMOSTANOLONE PROPIONATE)

Masteron is mainly used in the last four weeks prior to a contest. It does not appear to aromatise or cause water retention, neither is it liver toxic. It will however only benefit an athlete with extremely low body fat, it's use will provide a hard and ripped look come contest time. If the body fat levels are too high the athlete will look smooth and flat. Works well with Primobolan, Winstrol and Oxandrolone to harden a low fat physique.

Dosage would be 100mg injected every other day,

Side effects might include hair loss and acne.

MEGAGRISEVIT (CLOSTEBOLE ACETATE)

This steroid comes in a two-pack of 1.5 ml vials, which also contain vitamin B6 & B12. The 2 vials are usually mixed before injecting. It is not a particularly strong or effective steroid, neither is it convenient to use or easily available. Used as an addition to a stack you may see results, used on it's own you may be disappointed.

Dosage is usually the combined 3ml/20mg jab daily.

METHANDRIOL DIPROPRIONATE (METHYLANDROSTENEDIOL DIPROPIONATE)

To be taken in either tablet or oil based injectable form. It is a strong anabolic, which is also accompanied by a highly androgenic effect, although it does not exhibit water retention any more than Deca. By itself the drug isn't particularly impressive however when taken in conjunction with other steroids it really starts to come into it's own. It allows high absorption of other steroids into the receptor cells thus enhancing the effects of other steroids being used. It is mainly found as part of a compound in Veterinary steroids such as Drive, Spectriol and Geldabol. It is slightly toxic and an anti-estrogen is recommended.

The oil-based dosage is usually 100mg every 2-3 days, the daily dose for the oral version is 40-60 mg, spread into 3 doses.

It is slightly liver toxic and side effects may include, stomach pains, high blood pressure, acne and gynecomastia.

METHYBOL – SEE DECA

METHYLTESTOSTERONE

This substance is the most basic form of testosterone known. The majority of the substance is destroyed by the liver and its half life is less than 1hr. It's fast in and fast out, it gives a huge aggression kick and is mainly used by strength athletes before a lift. It is also used a lot by counterfeiters who try and pass it off as Dianabol.

Methyltestosterone could be used as a training booster, however it will exhibit no permanent strength or weight gains. Couple that with the fact that it is extremely liver toxic and will bring out your acne, water retention and gyno' in a flash, and there seems to be very little point to this item at all.

NILEVAR

Nilevar is a weak compound that has very mild muscle building effects, it does increase water retention somewhat and this is usually the main cause for any increase in body weight whilst using it.

Dosage is 30-40mg per day for no more that 4-6 weeks, it is liver toxic and will produce the usual side effects such as acne, high blood pressure etc.

NOLVADEX (TAMOXIFEN CITRATE)

Nolvadex/Tamoxifen is an anti-estrogen, which is commonly used to combat breast cancer. Most of the side effects associated with highly androgenic compounds can be somewhat reduced by the use of Nolvadex.

The way this works is by competing with steroids for the estrogen receptors, the flip side to this coin is that by reducing the side effects it also reduces the effectiveness of the steroid as an anabolic.

Tamoxifen will also promote fat loss as part of a diet, by keeping estrogen low, and will promote hardness in a lean physique.

Dosages are usually in the range of 10-20mg per day. This compound is highly recommended for people using highly androgenic steroids such as Dianabol, Anadrol and Testosterone.

NUBAIN

An opiate based compound, with little or no use at all in real body building terms. Apparently it is an anti-catabolic, however it is widely reputed, due to it's opiate base, to be addictive. This item has ruined many a good bodybuilder, and more besides. Steer clear, its worthless.

OMNADREN 250 (TESTOSTERONE: PHENYLPROPRIONATE, PROPRIONATE, ISOHEXANOATE AND HEXANOATE)

A blend of four testosterones blended in the same way for example Sustanon 250 but with different compounds. This drug is a far more pronounced and harsh drug than Sustanon. It has higher water retention properties and will promote body weight increase quite rapidly (usually the water). It also promotes acne and aggression slightly more than Sustanon.

Omnadren is quite cheap and is often re-labelled as Sustanon, at a higher price of course. The usual dosage is a single 250mg shot per week.

ORABOLIN (ETHYLESTRENOL)

Orabolin is a weak compound which is not particularly effective when used on it's own. It does not have many side effects and will only increase liver values if taken in high doses over a prolonged period. If used as part of a stack with compounds such as Winstrol, Masteron and Parabolin it will promote gains that are substantial and will remain after the course has ended.

Dosages are usually 20-40mg daily.

ORAL-TURINABOL

If this product were still commercially available I would be happy to go into great depth regarding its worth as an anabolic substance. The fact is that the only company that did produce it commercially, Jenapharm Gmbh stopped production of this item years ago. Unless it has been commercially re-introduced any packs floating about will be fakes, if they work its probably because they contain another more readily available compound.

OXANDROLONE SPA (A.K.A. ANAVAR)

Anavar is primarily an anabolic not an androgenic compound. Whilst considered to be a mild steroid it's users report that most of the gains made during its use are kept after discontinuation of the product. Its biggest gains can be seen in strength increases. It promotes muscle hardness and stacks well with just about any steroid, Dianabol for bulking, Clenbuterol for fat burning and Andriol for the cautious user.

It has very little if at all any side effects. It does not shut down the body's own testosterone production, does not aromatise, does not cause premature bone closure and is not considered to be toxic. Although it is 17-alpha alkylated and will therefore increase liver values if taken in high does over prolonged periods. It has been known to give a feeling of fullness or discomfort in the stomach.

Dosages are usually 8 – 12of the 2.5 mg tabs per day. The manufactures recommended dosage is 0.125mg per pound of body weight (adults).

PARABOLAN (TRENBOLONE HEXAHYDROBENCYLCARBONATE)

Made by Negma in France from 1980 onwards, it is the shorter acting, human version, of Finaject. Parabolan is a strong, highly anabolic and highly androgenic steroid. Its use will result in rapid and high quality muscle gains. In a slightly different manner, it is a highly effective androgen but without the usual aromatisation characteristics of an androgen. It does not aromatise and does not promote water retention. This is an ideal steroid to use for contests; it will promote a hard, vascular and ripped look in a dieting athlete whilst protecting the body from over training whilst on reduced calories.

The only note of caution with Parabolan is that courses should not last longer than 6-8 weeks. Parabolan is quite toxic, mainly putting stress on the Kidneys, not the liver. It is important that athletes consume an additional 3-4 litres of water per day in order to flush out the kidneys.

Also note that Parabolan is widely counterfeited, most people who report less than satisfactory results are probably using a fake. The original French product is packaged individually, one to a box in a 76mg per 1.5 ml ampoule. Each ampoule is also packed with it's own individual ampoule saw, which is in plastic wrapping. The ampoules have red print on them, which is raised the expiry date is vertical. The print should not be easy to remove or scrape off. The original ampoules have exactly 1.5ml of oil in each, no more, no less.

Dosages are usually in the range of 1 ampoule every 3 days.

Side effects are minimal although it will put stress on the kidneys and can increase aggression, due to the high androgen content.

PERIACTIN (CYPROHEPTADINE HYDROCHLORIDE)

Basically this is an antihistamine that can be used to increase your appetite, dosages around 4-8mg per day. Can cause drowsiness.

PERMASTRIL – SEE MASTERON

ORAL PRIMABOLAN (METHENOLONE ACETATE)

Originally available in 5, 25 and 50mg tablets, now only the 25 mg is available, the others have not been produced for some time.

Primobolan is an extremely high anabolic and a very low androgen compound. It is not as harsh on the liver as other oral compounds and does not promote water retention or other side effects associated with androgens, although hair loss may occur if such a predisposition exists.

Whilst being a comparatively safe steroid to take it is not

incredibly effective in promoting rapid gains in muscle mass or strength. The gains that are made will be kept after discontinuation of the drug. Steroid novices or women athletes mainly use this compound.

Primobolan can be useful to the male athlete at contest time as it has fat burning capabilities, although it shouldn't be the only drug used as muscle loss may occur due to it's mildness.

Theories exist that localised fat loss can be promoted by grinding a 25mg tablet into a fine powder and mixing it into half a teaspoon of DMSO gel. The gel can then be applied to areas where fat needs to be reduced. Do not rub the gel in but merely apply it. DMSO gel is the gel, which is present in ointments used to treat swellings and sports injuries.

Oral dosages for men are usually in the range of 100 - 200 mg daily, women use 50-100mg.

Side effects are minimal and Primobolan is appreciated by the more health conscious steroid user.

PRIMABOLAN DEPOT (METHENOLONE ENANTHATE)

Obviously this is the injectable version of the previously described oral compound. The oral version is taken daily; the injectable is usually taken weekly. The injectable version will produce slight water retention, which will result in the build up of strength and muscle, this water retention does not occur in the oral and therefore the injectable is considered slightly more effective.

Primobolan depot is favoured by health conscious athletes, it will not effect the body's own testosterone production and does not increase liver values. A stack of 400mg per week Deca,

200 mg per week Primobolan and 240mg per day Andriol is a very safe way to build satisfactory results. None of the above will significantly effect the bodies own testosterone production or damage the liver, unless of course you up the dosage over a prolonged period.

Dosages are usually around 200mg per week and side effects are minimal.

PROVIRON (MESTEROLONE)

Proviron is a high androgen with no anabolic effect and is non-toxic. This item is not used for the build up of muscle but is used to prevent some of the side effect associated with steroid use. Proviron is an estrogen antagonist, which will prevent the aromatisation of steroids. Gyno and water retention can be blocked my use of this item it will also promote a look of hardness in the muscle.

Uses for Proviron in Bodybuilding are limited, there are other drugs, which are better for the same purpose and are more easily available. A lot of athletes also use Proviron for contest prep as it promotes a look of hardness in the muscle, Clenbuterol (if used correctly) can produce a similar look. Proviron can be taken for a number of weeks with little or no side effects; it does not affect liver values. Male athletes who do want to use this drug for contest prep or as an anti estrogen usually use 50mg per day orally.

STEN (TEST PROPIONATE, TEST CYPIONATE, DIHYDROTESTOSTERONE) 120mg

Often compared to Sustanon, but actually a slightly different blend of testosterones. It is very similar in action to Sustanon,

however at half the mg dosage per ampoule you will need twice as many.
See Sustanon for more info.

STENBOLONE (ANATROFIN) 25-100mg/ml

An excellent choice whilst dieting, it helps build up the red blood cell count enormously and also helps the body recover and regenerate during a low calorie period. It is not liver toxic, not androgenic and does not aromatise.

Stenbolone made by the same company that makes Anadrol although it has no where near the bodybuilding potential of Anadrol in terms of mass building. It can be used for a slow progressive and solid gain in strength and muscle, usually preferred by the more cautious user. This compound has a short half-life and therefore requires frequent injections. The usual dosage is a 50mg (1ml) injection per day. Side effects are low.

SUSTANON 250 (TEST PROPIONATE, PHENYLPROPIONATE, ISOCAPROATE, DECONATE) 250mg/ml

Sustanon is a blend of four different testosterones, fast, medium and slow acting. It is effective within one day and remains active for up to 4 weeks. For Bodybuilding purposes a shot would be taken at least once per week, usually though 2-3 shots per week are used. This drug stacks well with just about any other compound. It is an outstanding anabolic, highly androgenic and will produce rapid gains in both strength and mass. It doesn't however produce as much water retention or aromatisation as the other testosterones.

Sustanon is a quality piece of kit and is often combined with Dianabol and Deca for bulking or Parabolan and Primobolan for quality. It's highly counterfeited and done quite well at that. An awful lot of the fakes are difficult to spot, more so than any other fake I've seen. Look for quality packaging and labels, package inserts etc. Most of the fakes are just a cheaper testosterone, usually a short acting one.
Get hold of a quality supply of Sustanon and you'll be a happy camper.

Although side effects are somewhat less than the other testosterones, the use of Nolvadex and HCG are still recommended. The other side effects still apply, acne, oily skin, aggression sexual stimulation etc.

TESLAC

Teslac is an estrogen antagonist, which is used for the same reasons as Nolvadex/Tamoxifen, these compounds do the job better and cheaper than Teslac. It's very pricey and not readily available.

TESTOSTERONE ENANTHATE/CYPIONATE

Technically Cypionate and Enanthate are two different forms of testosterone altogether, however they are both taken in more or less the same dosage range and have much the same effect as each other. Most people cannot tell the difference between the two. Both steroids give huge gains in both size and strength, this comes along with all the usual effects of testosterone.

The other thing to note about these two items is the massive potential for abuse. The average dosage is between 200 –

800mg per week, even when stacked with other compounds. It is however not unheard of for athletes to take dosages of 1000-2000mg per day!!! The reason for these legendary mega doses is quite simply this…testosterone packs on size and strength like nothing else!

Sometimes the muscles can look watery, flat and the athlete can be puffy with a little extra fat, but that is why it is used mainly in the off season for bulking. This stuff really blows you up and gets you strong, but yes….as always, there's a catch. Like with any of the 'big' steroids, the better it works, the more side effects you're gonna get. If taken in a shrewd sensible manner, with the accompanying Nolvadex/Tamoxifen stack, it can produce good gains at sensible dosages, with a positive side effect/benefit ratio. Up the dosages and yes the gains will also go up, but not directly in proportion, but the side effects will rocket.

With mega dosages you may expect baldness, acne, 'roid rage, high blood pressure, testicular atrophy, increased estrogen and fat storage. For the novice I would always recommend the use of the more friendly Sustanon 250, for those who cannot get hold of Sustanon or need an extra kick…stay with the sensible dosages and keep cycles down to an 8 week max, minimum 6 weeks off.

TESTOSTERONE PROPIONATE

OK, take everything you just read about Cypionate and Enanthate and apply it to propionate. Testosterone is testosterone right? Wrong! This testosterone is in slightly different ether and therefore breaks down and becomes inactive much quicker. For this reason propionate is injected every 1 – 2 days, for most people at a dose of 100mg every 2 days seems to work best.

Users of Propionate also seem to hold less water than with the other testosterones. Because of the need to inject daily, propionate is not favoured as much as the other 'tests' but because it gets in and out of the system so rapidly it can be used in the first week of a cycle whilst waiting for longer acting, slower 'tests' to kick in.

i.e. have a shot of cyp + prop on day 1, repeat the prop twice in the first week only. This way the prop is working whilst the Cypionate or Enanthate is kicking in, cease use of the prop after week 1.

The use of slow and fast acting 'tests' is essentially how Sustanon works, but Sustanon can usually do a much better job, in more specific doses, cheaper and better.

TESTOSTERONE SUSPENSION

An aqueous suspension of testosterone, yup water not oil in this one. Fast in, fast out. Daily injections are required, some times it is injected 2-3 times daily, which is a problem as it is painful to inject and you end up feeling like a pincushion.

It is not widely used by amateurs, for good reason, there are many other more pleasant and productive chemicals to use. It is some times used in a mega dose by power lifters on the day of a contest for some last minute explosive action.

Another application that has been known is to use it in the last week before a bodybuilding contest. Suspension is said to promote glycogen storage in the muscle, therefore a dosage of 50-100mg per day pre contest can help with carb loading and lead to tight, hard looking muscles.

All side effects of the other testosterones apply.

TESTOSTERONE HEPTYLATE THERAMEX

An effective European testosterone, both highly androgenic and anabolic. Said to be stronger at the same dosage than the previously listed testosterones with less water retention. Usually taken in dosages of 250mg, 2-3 times per week. A real alternative where Sustanon is not available, much preferred over the other testosterones, although you don't generally see much of it about. Look for the ampoules in the double packs.

TESTOVIRON DEPOT

This product is rarely found and is actually only a combination of testosterone Enanthate and propionate. Nothing special, check out the previous listings of these two items for further information.

TESTOSTERONE UNDECONATE

Simply another name for Andriol – see earlier listing.

TRIACANA (TIRATRICOL)

Triacana is simply a weaker relative of Cytomel. It usually comes in 0.35 mg tablets and dosages range from 10 – 20 tablets per day, in four separate dosages. It is sometimes stacked with Clenbuterol and/or other fat burners in order to increase its effect. Dosage inaccuracies can be tolerated slightly better than with the more brutal Cytomel. It is a good beginners choice stacked with Clenbuterol, rather than jumping straight in with Cytomel.

WINSTROL (STANOZOLOL)

Available in 2 and 5 mg tablets, not very much else to say about this, not positive anyway. It is said to be a weak steroid in low dosages, and in high dosages in can cause upset stomachs and liver stress. Few people have reported gains on this item; those that do say it is a quality gain, not an easy item to use. Dosages for men range from 24 – 50mg per day, half that for women. If your body can tolerate the higher dosages you may benefit from using Winstrol.

WINSTROL V (DEPOT INJECTION)

This is a fast acting water-based steroid that requires painful daily injections. It will not provide huge gains in size or strength but can be used pre-contest to 'cut up' and achieve harder looking muscle. It is a low androgen and therefore does not induce water retention, great news at contests!

The other use for this item, apparently, is for site injections. Lagging body parts such as biceps, triceps, delts and calves can be 'perked up' by localised, daily site injections. This is thought to be a result of a build up of scar tissue behind the muscle as opposed to quality growth.

Strictly speaking this item is a veterinary steroid, usually manufactured in a multi use vial. The genuine article has a milky white solution which, when left to settle, separates – clear solution at the top, milky white particles at the bottom. The genuine multi use vial will appear 2/3 clear and 1/3 milky when settled. The fakes are in reverse and have only 1/3 clear solution at the top. If you find this stuff in ampoules or vials only accept the 1ml version.

Side Effects

Each and every steroid has it's own benefits and it's own problems. No such thing as the 'perfect steroid' exists, although some are better than others. If your ethos is 'I want to grow and to hell with the damage' then your use or misuse of the drugs will decide your fate. A more analytical and cautious approach would be the best way forward. Make an informed decision and always monitor your progress/side effect ratio before proceeding to the next level. The strange thing being of course is that everyone is different, one man can take 10 Anadrol per day no problem, and the next will have Liver strain with only 3 Dianabol tablets. I don't wish to scare monger, or create paranoid athletes, however there are no certainties when it comes to side effects and tolerance levels, so caution is the key word.

ACNE

This side effect will occur in most steroid users, although to varying degrees. People who have high sebum gland receptors will suffer the most. The general rule of thumb is that the more androgenic a steroid is, the more acne it will produce. The androgens increase oil production is the sebum gland, causing greasy skin, combine this with the toxins in the blood from the steroids and you have an environment rife for spots. Use of Retin A or Accutane can help alleviate the worst of acne but can cause dryness of the skin and eyes.

ATROPHY OF THE TESTES

The external introduction of testosterone (steroids) will cause the body to temporarily shut down its own testosterone production in the testes. This will obviously result in temporary size shrinkage of the nuts. One way to help this problem is the use of HCG during and after the cycle to keeps your nuts in action. Andriol and Anavar do not have a negative effect on the bodies own testosterone productions.

BLEEDING

Steroids can cause an increase in blood pressure, this can manifest itself in nosebleeds. The nosebleeds can also be difficult to stop because steroids also cause a slight thinning of the blood, which in turn increases clot time. It would always be a good idea to cease using any steroids before medical operations.

BONE CLOSURE

With the exception of Anavar most other steroids will cause premature bone closure in teenagers. As we grow our bones grow in length and thickness, when our bodies have finished growing, usually age 18-22 our bone ends close up. If steroids are used by a person who has not yet reached his full height potential, the closing of the bone ends will cause a premature height deficiency. This is a permanent and irreversible feature. The general rule of thumb would be to refrain from steroid use during your pubescent/teenage years, 21 years of age would be the earliest point of use.

ENLARGED CLITORIS

Also known as 'King Prawn' an enlarged clitoris can be unsightly, although not harmful. Increased androgens are the culprit for this side effect, the enlarged clitoris, although unsightly, can help a women achieve orgasm easier. This is due to the increase in both size and thus sensitivity.

ERECTIONS

The usual trend would be that at the beginning of the cycle when steroids are first used, your body is still producing it's own testosterone, thus frequent erections occur. Further into the cycle as the bodies own testosterone decreases and eventually shuts down, erections and sexual desire decrease. At the end of a cycle there is a testosterone 'lull' between the last shot/pill wearing off and the bodies own testosterone production starting. At this point erections and sexual desire can be non-existent. This is why HCG is again recommended both during and after a cycle, to keep testosterone production on the move and to help re-start the testes after a cycle.

GYNECOMASTIA

Excess androgens in your system, from steroids, will convert into the female hormone estrogen. This will cause a build up of fatty tissue in the breast/nipple area and it is usually quite sore. This tissue build up is referred to as 'bitch tits' or 'boy boobs', upon discontinuation of the steroids soreness and tissue size will reduce slightly, only to re-appear with a vengeance during the next course. The use of Tamoxifen, during and after a cycle can help reduce and sometimes even avoid this side effect all together.

HAIRLOSS

Again the more powerful compounds are tainted with the most side effects. The high androgen steroids will also predominantly have a high conversion rate to DHT. This will in turn trigger male pattern baldness, the more androgens, the higher DHT conversion, the greater the hair loss. Some hair growth will occur after steroid use is discontinued, however assume that it will be a mainly permanent feature.

HEADACHES

If you suffer persistent headaches always check with your doctor for other causes. In the case of steroid use headaches can be caused by hormonal imbalance and/or increased blood pressure. Assume that highly androgenic items are at the worst end of the scale for this problem.

HEARTDISEASE

Steroids can cause an increase in cholesterol, combine this with weight gain, and high blood pressure and you've got a time bomb on your hands. Tamoxifen/Nolvadex can help reduce this side effect and as always is recommended. Keep an eye on your diet, fat levels and cholesterol levels, it'll help reduce any risks before they occur.

HYPERTENSION

As mentioned, quite frequently, increased blood pressure is a common side effect of steroids use. Hypertension can cause all sorts of problems from bleeding to artery problems and strokes. Keep an eye on your blood pressure during and after cycles, the use of Tamoxifen/Nolvadex is recommended, also keep an eye on your fat and water levels, it all adds up.

JAUNDICE/LIVER PROBLEMS

Anyone who suffers with prior kidney or liver problems should either consult their doctor or avoid steroid use altogether. Predominantly Liver/Kidney problems are a result of steroid abuse as opposed to steroid use. The prolonged use of steroids at high dosages will put a tremendous strain on your system and whilst the Liver is a self-regenerating organ it can only take so much abuse. Avoid alcohol and other medication whilst on gear, if you get yellow skin, the white of your eyes turn yellow of you get a swollen and painful Liver….stop taking gear and see a doctor ASAP!

ROID RAGE

As with anything in life you only know when you've had enough…..when you've had too much. Reasonable dosages of the less drastic steroids, say for example deca, shouldn't really cause any noticeable effects. Where as high dosages of high androgens such as Testosterone and Anadrol would be more likely to cause problems. Think of it this way, you increase in size, strength and weight, somewhere along the line there is an increase in attitude. Combine this with a hormonal imbalance and increased male aggression and you might have a problem. Keep your reality in check, make sure you control the gear, don't let it control you.

STOMACH ACHES OR FULLNESS

Anavar has been known to cause stomachaches in some people, it's a nice steroid in most other ways so if you don't get any problems with it your lucky. Anadrol has been known to cause feelings of fullness and/or nausea, probably due to it being such a powerful compound. This side effect doesn't occur in everyone, it's more a tolerance thing.

VIRILIZATION

This is really a problem for the ladies. If a female takes a male hormone, even in small quantities, she will inevitably suffer some male characteristics as a side effect. Problems such as thinning of the hair, deeper voice, hairiness enlarged clitoris etc may manifest them selves. Again high androgens are the main cause, sticking with the low androgens and high anabolics will not make you immune but it will help.

WATER RETENTION

A small amount of water retention can help with bodybuilding, it can swell the muscles and cushion the joints, it can also help with the transfer of nutrients to the muscles. The moon face or puffy look is usually a sign of water retention. Heavy water retention is however a problem and can be a sign of a more serious problem such as high blood pressure. Nolvadex can help with this problem, keep a low salt diet to reduce sodium levels.

Counterfeits

Yes, the problem of counterfeits, not a very interesting issue but a very important one. Counterfeits are basically copies of the original item, usually made by an illegal lab. The problem with this is that you cannot guarantee the contents, quality or cleanliness/sterility of the drug you are using (or think you are using).

For example, do we think that the hygiene standards of an underground lab are to be compared to that of a major manufacturer…probably not? If a legitimate item states it has 100mg per ml then chances are that's what's in it, can we guarantee the dosage of an underground lab….Probably not? If the bottle from a legit company says its got deca in, chances are, it's deca. Can an illegal lab guarantee it has the right contents in…. probably not?

So it's simple, yes? Don't but from an illegal source? Ahem, not quite so simple. Steroids cannot be purchased legally without a doctor's prescription, so there is no such thing as a legal supply. On top of this, the underground labs don't announce the fact that it's a fake product on the label, they actually copy the original item. Some times a shabby copy is very evident, however today's manufacturing techniques aren't exactly cutting edge and can be easily copied. Thus a fake item and a real item can be practically indistinguishable.

Here are some good pointers to use as a general rule of thumb.

Steer clear of multi use vial and tablets sold loose, always insist on a packaged product. Most vials and ampoules will come in cardboard boxes packed as singles or in packs of 3. Look for detailed and quality package inserts, as most legitimate items will have a product description, dosage and side effects list inserted.

Avoid low quality packaging and squiffy labels, look for professional packaging and package inserts. Labels should fit properly and be straight with clear print. Watch out for dodgy vials with loose or hand crimped stoppers. Ampoules should be perfectly formed and symmetrical, not wonky or badly formed. Any ampoules without paper labels should be screen-printed so that the print cannot be rubbed or scratched off easily.

In particular pay very close attention to the expiry dates and lot numbers, all steroids should have them on both the product (i.e. on the vial label or foil strips for tablets) as well as the packaging (the cardboard box they come in). If the expiry dates and lot numbers are printed in the same ink as the rest of the box or label then you've got a problem. This is because the fakers usually print large quantities of boxes and labels at one time, thus they all have the same ink as the rest of the writing on the label/box. The legit' item would have the date either printed/stamped on separately or more likely embossed into the cardboard box or foil strips. This is because the legit source is required by law to print exact and up to date expiry information on each item they produce, where as the counterfeiters just print off batch quantities. The internet can be a good place to dig up information and images of fakes vs. legit examples.

Orals and Injectables

Orals and injectables.... what's the difference. Well there's the obvious answer of 'one you swallow, one you inject' But let's be more specific.

Orals are generally harsher on your body than injectables, there's always an exception to the rule, but generally this is the case. The reason for this is that when you take an oral administration of a chemical that is foreign or toxic to your body, the first thing your body wants to do is destroy it and then excrete it. As the tablet/chemicals travel through the gastrointestinal tract and then to the liver it would normally be destroyed. To prevent this happening scientist added a carbon atom, to the 17th carbon position of the steroid compound, to protect it from destruction by the liver. This process stops the liver breaking it down, but then also this process is harsh on the liver. The higher the milligram dosage of steroid the harsher the effects on the liver.

Most oral steroids are C17 or Alpha Alkylated as described as above, with the exception of one or two. Andriol is not, it takes a different route of absorption into the body and therefore places little or no stress at all on the liver. The others are Orabolin and Primabolin tablets, Orabolin is not considered to be an effective or worthwhile steroid, Primabolin tablets are no longer available.

Orals are usually destroyed completely by the liver within 24hrs and therefore require daily dosages. Also you will usually find that the more harmful a steroid is....the more powerful it is.

Injectables are not made for intra-venous administration (into the vein) they are made for intra-muscular administration (into the muscle) this way they miss out the pass through the intestine and liver. Some of the harsher or cruder items, especially in large doses will put strain on the kidneys. A large area like the buttocks, thigh or delts is preferred as an injection site, buttocks being the number one choice due to there being fewer veins and nerves to hit.

The two choices for injection are water based or oil based steroids. Water based are fast in and fast out, administer every day or so. Oil based steroids are slower into the system and longer lasting, administered usually once or twice weekly. This is why an injectable item such as Sustanon works so well, it is a blend of fast, medium and slow release testosterones, thus gives an even and timely dosage release.

Most orals will promote creatine phoshate systhesis which will encourage strength gains more significantly than injectable steroids. The use of injectables is usually less stressful on the body overall.

How to Inject

The two most commonly used needles are colour coded as 'greens' and 'blues'. The green is a 1.5" needle, which is predominantly used for oil-based injections, such as deca. The second needle is the 'blue' a slightly thinner and shorter needle for water based injections, such as HCG. A third needle is sometimes used, an insulin needle, and is the shortest and thinnest needle, it is used for subcutaneous injections of items such as insulin.

The technique for an injection of an oil-based steroid is as follows. Flick the vial or ampoule to be used with a snap of the wrist to ensure that all of the oil is at the bottom of the container. On ampoules hold the ampoule firmly and, with a firm movement, break the top off. Don't hold too tightly or you'll crush the glass, break it off with a clean snap. File a groove into the neck before snapping off, if necessary, a file is usually provided if this is the case.

Place a needle onto the syringe and insert into the neck of the ampoule, gently but firmly draw all of he oil into the syringe. If you are using a vial with a rubber stopper, before inserting the syringe, draw air fully into the syringe, insert into the rubber stopper then depress the air into the vial. This will create enough air pressure in the vial to assist with filling the syringe. At this point, when the air is in the vial, push the needle to the bottom and the plunger should raise, drawing the oil into the chamber, draw any remaining oil into the syringe manually.

After the syringe is full remove it from the vial/ampoule. At this point your needle will probably be dull from pushing through the rubber stopper and grinding on the bottom of the glass vial/ampoule. Replace the needle with a fresh sharp one. Gently push the oil fully to the top of the needle so you can see a small amount of oil dribble down the needle, also give the syringe chamber a quick flick to loosen and eliminate any small air bubbles. At this point you are ready for the jab.

The area into which you should inject is the glute (buttock muscle) it is a large area to miss, fairly numb, and has fewer veins and nerves to hit. Either side will do, the area to aim for is as follows. As you look at your 'cheek' face on, mentally dissect it into equal quarters. Choose the center spot of the upper, outer quarter that is closest to the hip.

With your free hand, stretch the skin of the injection area with your index finger and thumb. Try to place your weight on the opposite leg to the side you are injecting. Also try to keep the muscle loose, take a moment to breath and relax before you inject to ensure it is as relaxed as possible. Then hold the syringe firmly in your other hand, similar to a dart, and insert into the buttock. This should be done with one swift flick, try not to either, ease it in bit by bit nor stab furiously. You can practise a couple of times on an orange or tangerine to get the feel and technique right.

Also, and this might sound fairly basic, but watch what you are doing. I once had a friend that couldn't bear to do his own jabs, one week he had to do the jab himself, closed his eyes at the crucial point…..he stabbed himself in the thumb. What a tit.

Once the needle is in place, gently, slowly and firmly inject the oil into the buttock. If the oil comes out of the sides you didn't inject deep enough. When done, wait for 5 seconds or so just to let things settle down, at this point draw the needle out SLOWLY. I was in a rush once and pulled the needle out too quickly….gush, a large spurt of blood shot across the bathroom floor and took a while to stop. Quite strange to see, but could have been avoided with a little patience. After you withdraw the needle press firmly on the injection site for a minute or so with some cotton wool or loo roll to absorb any blood and keep things clean.

That's it, job done, alternate buttocks between shots. Delts and quads can be used but glutes are best. The process is the same for water based injections with blues, but water based injections always seem to sting more….maybe that's just me though!

To avoid abbesses and infections, always use clean needles, never re-use and never share. Avoid multi use vials as bacteria can breed on the stopper. An alcohol swab can be used to clean the injection area both before and after. It's not a bad idea to use your local needle exchange, you get free, clean needles, swabs and a recycling tube!

Stacks and Cycles

Steroids can be used either on their own or as part of a 'stack' whereby a number of different compounds can be used in various ways to get the best effect. One benefit of stacking is that multiple items can be used in smaller dosages to gain better effects than a single item in large dosages. Another reason is that certain items can work in synergy with each other to produce fantastic results.

Steroids are also used in a cycle method, whereby you will use the drugs for a set period, usually 4 – 12 weeks and then have an off period. The off period is usually as long as the cycle you just finished.

There are a number of reasons for cycling steroids, the main ones are as follows. The steroid receptors in your body can become closed to the steroids in as little as 3 weeks. Cycling the steroids helps to keep the receptors open. In order to continue getting results you can either up the dosage or change the drug. An off period allows the receptors to re-open. Another reason to cycle steroids is to give your body a rest from the stress being placed on the liver and kidneys. Predominantly the stress on the liver and kidneys comes from orals, items such as Anadrol should be on a 4-6 week course max.

STACK EXAMPLES

There are a variety of theories as to which stack and cycle combinations work best, presumably this is more dependant on your needs, goals and cash! A stack, which is known as the diamond pattern, has been popular for a number of years, this is outlined below. Take it as read that Nolvadex is recommended for the duration of all stacks and HCG is required at the end of the stack.

Week 1: 200mg Deca + 20mg Dianabol

Week 2: 200mg Deca + 30mg Dianabol

Week 3: 200mg Deca + 40mg Dianabol

Week 4: 400mg Deca + 50mg Dianabol

Week 5: 400mg Deca + 50mg Dianabol

Week 6: 400mg Deca + 50mg Dianabol

Week 7: 400mg Deca + 50mg Dianabol

Week 8: 200mg Deca + 40mg Dianabol

Week 9: 200mg Deca + 30mg Dianabol

Week 10: 200mg Deca + 20mg Dianabol

Deca is injected weekly, orals taken daily.

The benefit of the diamond stack is that the body receives a steady influx of steroids over a set period that produces good gains and tapers off well, thus reducing a post cycle crash. After the cycle is complete a 10-week off period would be recommended. This cycle can then be used 2-3 times per year. One school of thought on the negative side is that the lower dosages at the beginning of the cycle allow the receptors to close up early on, therefore reducing the effectiveness of the higher dosages later on in the stack. In order to combat this, a stack that lasts only 4 –5 weeks would be used, however you would go straight in at full dosage, and taper of in the last week only.

Example:

Week 1:   **400mg Deca + 50mg Dianabol**

Week 2:   **400mg Deca + 50mg Dianabol**

Week 3:   **400mg Deca + 50mg Dianabol**

Week 4:   **400mg Deca + 50mg Dianabol**

Week 5:   **200mg Deca + 50mg Dianabol**
(start 50mg Monday, reducing by 5mg each day until last day of week.)

Deca is injected weekly, orals taken daily.

This way, the receptors get the full benefit of the full dosage for the duration of the stack. The receptors will not have shut down completely, and the off period is only 5 weeks. This way, productive stacks can be repeated 5-6 times per year.

An alternative, yet similar theory can be used called the 3-week blitz. This stack uses a single compound at a time, at max dosage, for only 3 weeks, overlapping on the last week. See below.

Week 1:   **400mg Deca**

Week 2:   **400mg Deca**

Week 3:   **400mg Deca + 50mg Dianabol**

Week 4:   **50mg Dianabol**

Week 5:   50mg Dianabol + 500mg Sustanon

Week 6:   500mg Sustanon

Week 7:   500mg Sustanon + 300mg Primobolan

Week 8:   300mg Primobolan

Week 9:   300mg Primobolan

The above lists are various ways to cycle the steroids, the other consideration is which items to put together.

Example, for bulking, the use of Anadrol and Testosterone Cypionate would work rapidly. A more cautious approach to the same means would be Dianabol and Sustanon. For slower, but more solid gains with less water, perhaps Primobolan and Parabolan Depot together.

A very safe stack would be Andriol and Anavar, perhaps with a small amount of Primobolan. Again not a rapid mass building stack, but quality gains with very few side effects.

Deca comes highly recommended in just about any situation, it stacks well with most items, as does Sustanon and Dianabol. These 3 items used in the 4-5 week repeat stacks are a particular favorite of mine.

The ways in which the steroids can be put together are endless, combining orals, injectables, high Androgen, low androgen, bulkers, cutters etc, etc, to gain the desired results, in the desired way.

Overleaf is an example of how a 4-5 week blitz can be combined with a bulking stack and then switched to a cutting/hardening stack. This one is a beauty.

Week 1: 400mg Deca + 500mg Sustanon + 50mg Dianabol

Week 2: 400mg Deca + 500mg Sustanon + 50mg Dianabol

Week 3: 400mg Deca + 500mg Sustanon + 50mg Dianabol

Week 4: 400mg Deca + 500mg Sustanon + 50mg Dianabol

Week 5: 2500IU HCG (MON & THUR)

Week 6: 2500IU HCG (MON & THUR)

Week 7: 300mg Primobolan + 228mg Parabolan +30mg Anavar

Week 8: 300mg Primobolan + 228mg Parabolan + 30mg Anavar

Week 9: 300mg Primobolan + 228mg Parabolan + 30mg Anavar

Week 10: 300mg Primobolan + 228mg Parabolan + 30mg Anavar

Week 11: 2500IU HCG (MON & THUR)

Week 12: 2500IU HCG (MON & THUR)

Again, injectables listed are dosages per week, and orals per day. In the above bulking/hardening stack you get the best of both worlds. A 4-week switch to avoid receptor downgrade, a rapid bulking stack at high dosage influx and then a hardening cycle that still brings good gains and firms up earlier gains.

A good piece of kit also is Clenbuterol, to be used during cycles as a cutting agent or between cycles to minimise muscle loss.

As a final suggestion this is a nice mild, mid term stack which can be used. Quite low on side effects but good on gains. A nice starter and intermediate stack for the more cautious user.

Week 1:   200mg Deca + 15mg Dianabol + 120mg Andriol

Week 2:   200mg Deca + 20mg Dianabol + 160mg Andriol

Week 3:   200mg Deca + 25mg Dianabol + 200mg Andriol

Week 4:   200mg Deca + 30mg Dianabol + 240mg Andriol

Week 5:   200mg Deca + 25mg Dianabol + 200mg Andriol

Week 6:   200mg Deca + 20mg Dianabol + 160mg Andriol

Week 7:   1500iu HCG on Thursday

The above cycles and stacks are an insight into how the drugs can be combined and used. There are many, many more combinations and stacking methods available. The above examples are merely a small portion of that. Just about any cycle can be extended, shortened or chopped in half. Most of the drugs in the example stacks can be altered in dosage, up or down and even substituted completely for different compounds to get different effects.

Define your goals, i.e. bulking, hardening, cutting etc also decide on your time constraints and side effect sensitivity aspect. With these parameters in mind you can devise and implement a structured stacking/cycling system that will benefit your progress in the best manner for your personal situation. Always bear in mind that there is no definitive one system that works for all. Define your own goals and parameters before proceeding.

Coming off Steroids

At some point you are going to have to come off steroids, well, you don't have to……but it's a good idea. So the point where you let go needs to be planned, there are certain techniques that you can implement in order to make the best of the muscle you have gained and minimise any losses. Here are some pointers to bear in mind.

Enthusiasm and consistency should not reduce, for whatever reason some people only manage to find the enthusiasm to train properly when they are on steroids. This is a major mistake, firstly if you let your training slack off when you come off the gear then you are bound to lose muscle mass. Therefore remain consistent with your training after a stack. The other reason you should train properly during the off period is that the harder you train whilst off gear, the more likely you are to push your body closer to a catabolic state, this is when steroids would benefit you the most. So training hard and consistently between stacks will ensure you keep as much muscle as possible and also prepare your body for the next stack.

On the other side of the coin you must also be careful not to over train when you come off steroids, listen to your body. Anyone who has been upping the poundage's, sets and reps during a steroid cycle cannot expect these kinds of gains to continue whilst off the gear. To this end you must think about maintaining quality training, intensity and consistency, whilst noting when enough is enough. Always train to failure, but perhaps drop a set off each exercise. Your body will tell you when to slow down, if you listen and adjust your training you'll benefit. If you don't listen you'll either burn out or incur an injury.

Something else to consider at the end of a cycle is non-steroid anabolic and/or ant-catabolic items. Re-start you bodies own testosterone production with the use of HCG. Bearing in mind that as you set your testosterone off again you will incur a small rise in estrogens. Therefore the use of tamoxifen is recommended for 2-4 weeks after steroid use has finished. The use of tamoxifen during this period will keep estrogen levels down, whilst the HCG gets the body's hormone levels going, and will keep it sweet until everything balances out, thus maximising testosterone production and minimising estrogen production.

Think also about the way you taper your steroids, for example, if you have been on a heavy cycle for an extended period it would be extremely unwise to simply end the course, also known as cold turkey. The sudden stopping of steroids would cause a severe crash and the loss in muscle mass and motivation would be considerable. For this reason I would recommend that after a cycle you would taper off the steroids gently, reducing the dosages steadily. After a long course, say 12-14 weeks, had been used with high dosages, you would want to taper down over at least 2-3 of those weeks. If you were on a shorter course, say 4 weeks, on lower dosages a 1-2 week taper could be used. So, high dosages over a long period would call for a longer taper. Shorter stacks with lower dosages would be a shorter taper.

The introduction of an anti-catabolic, such as Clenbuterol, is also a good idea at the end of a stack. Clenbuterol is a great item and can be used a number of ways to your benefit. It can be used on a daily basis as a fat burner or on a 2 days on and 1 day off regime as an anti-catabolic muscle-building tool. See the separate information on Clenbuterol in the drug listings.

The intake of all your usual multi vitamin/mineral tablets is very important also, along with the use of any nutritional supplements you would normally use. If for example you have been using creatine, protein, MRP's and fat burners etc don't stop these when you stop your steroids, this would only make things worse. Your body will need all the assistance it can get, so make sure there is no slacking on either the training or nutrition. The use of anti-catabolics and fat burners, along with anti-estrogens, should ensure that most, if not all, off your hard earned gains would remain. You can expect to lose a couple of pounds of water, and maybe the weights you lift will suddenly seem a little bit heavier, maybe your reps will even drop a couple. But for the best results, both at the end of your current course and then during the next, remain consistent and positive regardless.

Eating to Grow

You are what you eat…..that's what they say, well, it's true, never more so than in bodybuilding. Also the flip side is that you can't be what you don't eat.

The body is put through tremendous strain during bodybuilding workouts, the physical exertion is phenomenal, therefore we need to fuel the body correctly. Think about it for a second, if you run an old 1.2 Vauxhall nova you don't need high quality fuel, or much of it. If you run a 6.2 formula 1 racing car, you're gonna need high octane fuel, lots of it, and it ain't cheap! Bodybuilding is the same, a pencil neck desk worker, with no physical demands can survive on only a bacon butty per day. You get a guy who has a physical job and then gets into bodybuilding and wham, you've got a serious carb, protein and overall calorie deficit.

The problem we have here is, as I stated earlier, you can't be what you don't eat, i.e. – if you don't eat big, you ain't gonna get big, end of story. You might get toned, you might get lean, but you ain't gonna get big. So what do we need?

As a bodybuilder we need to be looking at quality calories, and lots of them. We don't want to be pumping in loads of shite foods, full of sugars and fats, just in a vain attempt to up the calories, this is a false gain (probably fat and water). We need quality calories. Again with the calorie situation, it's the same as steroid situation, everyone is different. You're going to have to start with a base line and work up, I'd recommend a minimum of 3500 calories per day in order to grow. If this level of calories doesn't produce gains, then up it to 3750 and so on, until growth occurs. As your growth plateaus and stagnates, repeat as necessary. A hard training bodybuilder is going to need anywhere between 3500 and 5000 calories per day.

Obviously there are other things you can do to induce growth, shock principles, new course of steroids etc, but you can bet your bottom dollar that your nutrition is the best place to start. Most people overlook their nutritional requirements in a major way, much to their misfortune. Likewise when trying to lose weight, use this principal in reverse, find your calorie level which maintains a body weight and then reduce by a few calories, continue until weight loss occurs, and so on. You need to know what your own body needs and how to work with it.

One thing is for sure however, and that is that you need a vast amount of protein, we're talking 1.5 – 2 grams per pound of body weight. Therefore a 200pound male would need 300-400 grams of protein per day. Now there's no two ways about it, that's what you need and yes, it's a lot, but that's bodybuilding. Extreme training, extreme fuel and extreme growth - you can't do it by halves.

So how do you get this much protein, and this many calories? Well obviously you need to be looking at the best sources of quality protein and carbs. For your protein you should be eating, egg whites, fish, white meat, milk etc. Steer clear of sugary and fatty foods. Your carbs should come from rice, oats, wheat, pasta and fresh vegetables etc. The other way you can assist your diet is with the use of supplements, most people will struggle to get the necessary amount of calories and protein from regular food, and rightly so, you'd be eating non-stop. With the introduction of supplements you can really make your life a lot easier. For example, you may want to stick to your main 3 meals per day, and introduce the other 3 in the form of supplements. You could have breakfast as normal, say cereal, toast, porridge, juice etc, then mid morning take a meal replacement drink with a piece of fruit. Have your lunch as normal, say chicken breasts with baked potatoes, salad and a litre of water, then have a protein shake mid afternoon at about 2 or 3 o'clock. At about 4.30 – 5.00 have a pre-workout energy/carb drink . Post workout it is imperative that you take on board a high protein and carb drink exactly 45-60 minutes after your workout has ended. This is a valuable time slot, or window of opportunity, whereby you can refill your body's needs most effectively, your body will soak it up. At no later than 7-7.30 have your final meal of the day, eating large amounts late at night usually results in the food consumed being stored as fat. You can a have a light supper or a small snack before bed, to see your body through the night, a bowl of cereal and a banana work well to feed your body and stave of hunger induced insomnia, they also work in synergy to help induce sleep.

On the note of supplements, choose your brand carefully, always look for a recognised quality brand. If your paying under the odds the chances are that you'll get what you pay for. The topic of protein in particular also begs a few questions. There are various types of protein available, the two most controversial being Casein vs. Whey. Casein is a slow in and slow out form of protein, whey is a fast in and fast out form of protein. A lot of people have talked casein down based on this fact. Whey protein does also have a higher biological value (BV) than casein, which basically means that the body more easily absorbs it, but as I said, it's fast in and fast out. For this reason I tend not to favour either one or the other, I try to use them both. I always look for a protein or meal replacement drink that has BOTH casein and whey proteins included, not just one or the other. Also, don't think that avoiding cheap no-name brands means that you have to pay top dollar for everything, a lot of the major brands are available at great value prices by ordering from discount stores on the Internet. Again choosing your Internet store is like choosing your product, use a reputable one.

I also like to include the use of creatine, fat burners, ZMA, multi-vitamin/mineral tablets and 1-2 gms of vitamin C along side the protein drinks and meal replacement. If I'm gonna try and build a top-notch body, I gotta give it top notch nutrition….and plenty of it. I pretty much cycle my creatine use year round as the packet/tub recommends, maybe taking a full month out of every 12 off absolutely everything, as a complete body de-tox. Vitamin C is usually taken once or twice per day in the form of a 1000mg effervescent tablet, dissolved in half a pint of water. The Vitamin C really helps to keep the toxins flushed through and out of your system. It also helps keep the body's immune system in tip top condition, to help fight off infections like colds and flu etc. A good multi vitamin/mineral like Solgar VM-2000 should be taken daily as a matter of course to ensure there are no deficiencies in that area. The fat burners I like to use either with cutting stacks when I'm trying to harden things up a bit or between cycles, for the same reason.

If you find that you don't have the time to constantly prepare meals and protein drinks, it is a good idea to produce them in batches the night before. For example, if you are cooking Spaghetti Bolognese, instead of doing only 1 portion why not do 4, 5 or 6? You can freeze up the extra portions and defrost them later, maybe at home for tea or maybe at work for lunch. Why mix up only one protein drink? Mix 3 up the night before, let it chill in the fridge over night, have one for breakfast and take the other 2 to work with you in a flask. One for mid-afternoon and one for post workout. If you plan your meals and food preparation, even your supplements, you can really make a good job of getting the best foods down you in the easiest way possible. It just takes a little planning and thought, but once you get the rhythm going….it's a cinch! Bad planning will only lead to poor results. You can't leave anything to chance, plan your nutrition like you would plan your workouts and your stacks.

By using the information, in the manner described, you can combine your regular meals and your supplements to maximum benefit, this makes your day-to-day life as a bodybuilder much easier and fulfils your calorific and protein needs. Three large meals per day will not only be insufficient, but the large portions will cause bloating and sluggishness. Stick with the suggested food preparation methods described and you'll reap the results. Six smaller meals per day keeps your blood sugar more even, giving a smoother energy release, you'll also feel lighter and more sprightly. Make sure that you get the quality calories down you, use quality sources of protein and monitor your food intake in a conscious manner. Use a logbook if necessary to note your intake of calories, carbs, fats, proteins and sugars. This way you can see the direct trends and correlation between fat loss and muscle gain more effectively.

Training to Grow

As mentioned in a previous chapter, one of my pet hates is people that only see fit to train hard when they are on a course of steroids. In order to create the best growth environment possible you need to be consistent with your training. Persisting with on/off, half-hearted training will make for a sloppy and unhappy athlete, whilst stricter regimes will produce better results.

OK, so there's consistency to consider, what else? Sloppy technique, cheating, prolonged rest periods, insufficient intensity…..it's all there, every week when you trail down to the gym, it can all be observed. You'll see the guy who calls himself a gym rat just because he's there for 3 hours every night. Truth is, does he really have a 3 hours per night-awesome physique?? Not at all! He'll talk your bloody ears off all night, and then the first sign of working up a sweat and he hits the showers, avoid Mr Goby like the plague, he'll rob you of your training time. Then there's big guy, Tommy Tucker, in the corner curling with the mother of all weights, wow……NOT! Does he have a physique to aspire to? Nope. All that huffing and puffing, shouting and screaming, YES, YES, ONE MORE, C'MON!!! Who's he talking to exactly? Shouting at himself in the mirror as he sways violently backward and forward, swinging and heaving that ludicrous weight up and down. Please do not fall into the, more weight is better trap, train your muscles not your ego. Sloppy techniques are more likely to result in injuries than growth of any kind.

The way forward is brief, intense, controlled and planned workouts, using the correct form and technique. I'm a big fan of the Dorian Yates and Mike Mentzer style workouts. Although I must stress at this point, whilst I admire their workout style, we are not Mr Olympia's and therefore do not need to try and train as such. 20 set, twice per day, 7 days per week routines will not work for the average man. I recommend light reading such as Heavy Duty by Mike Mentzer and Brawn by Stuart Mc Robert. The idea behind this is figuring out what your body actually needs in order to grow, as opposed to over training unnecessarily.

So what are the basics? Well it has been established that the optimal number of reps, for body building purposes, is in the 5-9 region. If you can't manage 5 reps you've got too much weight on the bar. If you can do more than 10 reps, you need to add more weight. Any less than 5 reps and you're power lifting, any more than 9 and you're toning, so keep it in this range. Each body part should be trained fully and brutally only once per week, allowing at least 7 full days before hammering that body part again. Preferably split the body into 5 separate, brief and intense workouts, if you can't do 5 workouts per week , you can split it into 3. The theory that you should work on is to use incredibly strict form and technique, and progressive resistance.

So strict form, no bouncing the bar off the chest during a press, no swinging backwards and forwards during curls, no leaning over the bar on pushdowns etc. Each rep should be perfectly controlled by the muscle being worked and not the motion of body weight. On the negative part of the rep, i.e. lowering the bar in a bench press or curl, you should take 5-6 seconds to lower the bar, feeling the resistance all the way. Then smoothly, not jerking or rushing, start the positive motion, this would be pushing the bar back up, on the bench press, again, moving in a steady and defined manner. Breathe in on the negative and exhale firmly on the negative. At the top of the range, i.e. when the bar is at your chest in a curl, you should squeeze your muscle and hold the bar, feeling the muscle you are working fully contract. At the bottom, never fully lock out, keep constant tension on the muscle throughout. Recommended reading for this would be Stuart Mc Roberts – Insiders Tell all on weight training techniques, and /or Mike Mentzer Heavy Duty.

Progressive resistance? This means that we need to constantly challenge our body, to re-define our physical, and mental, boundaries. If we know that we can bench 120kg for 8 reps, for 4 sets and we continue to repeat that workout endlessly then we will simply stay at that level. In order to grow we need to take our body to a new level. By simply adding as little as 1 or 2 pounds to the bar each week, in a small space of time we can soon up the poundage's that our body can handle, with correct technique! With this new strength will come muscle growth, it's your body's way of coping with the stress. A valid comparison, as stated in the Arnold Schwarzenegger Encyclopaedia of bodybuilding is this: If a 12-horse power load is put on a 10-horse power motor, the motor burns out. If a 12-horse power load is put on a 10 horse power human body, the human body grows and becomes a 12-horse power body. With the correct, training, nutrition and rest this is exactly the case. So what this effectively means is that you need to constantly push your body to new limits …..progressive resistance!

Another consideration is what type of exercises are you going to do when you get to the gym? I recommend that you stick to the basics in order to grow. You know when you're down the gym, and there's some poor skinny guy pouring his heart and soul into his fifth set of calf raises or forearm curls, you gotta think to your self, what is he doing? If you haven't managed to build yourself a great set of quads, a thick chest, and a wide back then don't even think about messing around with endless sets of shaping exercises for the smaller muscle groups like calf raises and tricep extensions. You need to be doing the basic compound movements and building your strength up, deadlifts, bent over rows, squats, bench press, chins etc. Peaking your biceps, capping your delts and so on must come secondary to your first phase of bulk building. Once the major muscle groups are big, thick and strong then , and only then, should the shaping of smaller groups come into play.

So lets take a look at an example workout, a possible suggestion of a 3 or 5 day split.

5 day split:

Monday: Chest
Bench Press: 1-2 x warm up, 3 x sets
Incline Dmbl press: 2 x sets
Flat Flyes: 2 x sets

Tuesday: Legs
Squats: 1-2 x warm up, 4 x sets
Thigh Ext: 2 x sets
Ham Curl: 2 x sets
Calf Raise: 1 x set

Wednesday: Back
Bent over rows: 1-2 x warm up, 3 x sets
Deadlifts: 2 x sets
Wide Grip Pulldowns: 2 x sets

Thursday: Shoulders
Front Shoulder Press: 1-2 x warm up, 3 x sets
Dmbl Shrugs: 1 x sets
Side raise: 1 x sets
Rear bent over raise: 1 x sets

Friday: Arms
Bicep B/Bell curl: 1-2 x warm up, 3 x sets
Incline bicep curl: 1 x set
Tricep press: 3 x sets
Tricep ext: 1 x set

The idea behind the above workout is to get in the gym, warm up, hit your max weights and apply the previously discussed training techniques. No sloppy techniques, no rushing, no over training, just high intensity workouts. Get in the gym, go hard and go home. If 5 workouts per week proves to much you can link up some of the body parts to reduce the workouts to 3 per week, this is not as ideal but can work very well never the less.

3 day split:

Monday: Chest and Back
Bench Press: 1-2 x warm up, 3 x sets
Incline Flyes: 2 x sets
Bent over rows: 3 x sets
Wide Grip Pulldowns: 3 x sets

Wednesday: Legs
Squats: 1-2 x warm up, 4 x sets
Thigh Ext: 2 x sets
Ham Curl: 2 x sets
Calf Raise: 1 x set

Friday: Shoulders and Arms
Shoulder Press: 1-2 x warm up, 3 x sets
Side raise: 1 x sets
Rear bent over raise: 1 x sets
Tricep press: 2 x sets
Tricep ext: 1 x set
Bicep B/Bell curl: 2 x sets
Incline bicep curl: 1 x set

You will see from the previous examples that in all case a warm up need only apply to the first couple of sets of your first exercise, after that your body will be pumping blood at a sufficient rate to keep the rest of the muscles loose. You will also see on example 2, the 3 day split, where it was not possible to train each body part separately, certain body parts have been linked. Chest will be pushing exercises, back will be pulling. Chest will use the triceps, back will work the biceps. In both example, legs deserve a workout all of their own, legs are a major muscle group and growth in the quads can induce muscle growth throughout the whole torso. Do not neglect your quads, if anything give them more drive and attention than anything else, you'll feel the benefits in all your workouts.

On Shoulders, the triceps will fatigue and are moved before biceps. On the 3 day split, in all cases, except legs, the overall number of sets is reduced. This is because the body parts are now linked, and the body would not benefit from trying to maintain high set regimes all in one workout. Sets can be increased in the 5-day split, but must be reduced in the 3 day split to prevent over training. Keep your workouts as brief and intense as possible, workout for absolutely no longer than 50-60 minutes per session on the 3 day split and 30-40 minutes on the 5-day split. Limit rest periods between sets to a minimum of 30 seconds and a maximum of 60 seconds. Don't chat, don't get distracted, feel the muscle working and concentrate on giving 100% effort and concentration throughout your workout. The example workouts are based on the fact that you will give 100% on each and every set (except warm ups). Go to complete failure each time, DO NOT hold back in the earlier sets, thinking that you are saving something for a later set. Give your all, 100%, on each and every set, go to failure, go home, feed, rest and then come back next week and improve your best lift.

A final tip is visualisation. Pre-workout try and mentally picture yourself as a Herculean giant, breath deep, convince yourself that you'll lift more in this work out than ever before. Don't be mentally defeated before you even start your workout. Heading down to the gym with a 'I'm so tired' or 'I can't be bothered tonight, I'll just go through the motions' attitude is a waste of time. If you have been over training or perhaps you are unwell then it's essential that you rest, other than that, get your mind in check. Of course the weight will be heavy, of course it'll bear down on you like a tonne of bricks, but expand your chest, take a deep breath, block out negative thoughts and proceed like a warrior. Don't let the feel of the weights surprise you or quash you spirit, be prepared for the onslaught and focus on the job in hand. Don't hear anything or see anything else once you have the weights upon you, complete concentration for each and every rep of each and every set. Pay attention to timing, then when the job is done, congratulate yourself and forget about the workout. Don't sacrifice form or technique for weight, lift in a controlled and decisive manner and let your vision become a reality. Think big. Be big!

Terminology

Invariably whilst reading about steroids, and bodybuilding in general, or whilst talking to your buddies or the guys down the gym, you will come across terminology that you are unfamiliar with. In order that there is no confusion and that you use the information that you receive to your maximum benefit, I have outlined below a rough guide to common words and phrases associated with the said topics and explanations of what they mean. Avoid the classic classroom scenario where you stand nodding your head in a knowing fashion, whilst someone pontificates about a specific topic, only for you to then walk away wondering what the hell he/she was talking about, but felt to stupid to ask. Make sure the information you receive is properly understood and used in the correct context. See below for more info!

ANABOLIC:
This refers to the growth and building of muscular tissue, if something has an anabolic effect it means it is causing muscle growth.

ANDROGENIC:
This is a term used to explain secondary male characteristics such as deep voice, hair growth and sex drive etc. A steroid which is a high anabolic but low androgenic will produce muscle gains with few side effects, and vice versa. The biggest growth comes, unfortunately, from a high androgenic, high anabolic.

ANTI-CATABOLIC:
Catabolic is the reverse of anabolic, if your body is in a catabolic state it is in a state of decline. An anti-catabolic therefore refers to an item that reduces the body's catabolic signals.

AROMATISE:
When the body has high dosages of anabolic and androgenic steroids it will convert some of them into the female hormone estrogen. Some steroids convert more easily than others. When a steroid has aromatised, converted to estrogen, it can cause female characteristics such as bitch tits (see gynecomastia) and female orientated fat deposits (hips, breast). Nolvadex will reduce the aromatisation of a steroid, but therefore also slightly reduce its anabolic effect, an acceptable trade in my opinion.

ARRAY:
Array is another word for stack, example, if you are using an array of steroids, it simply means you are combining a number of different steroid items….a stack.

BITCH TITS:
See gynecomastia

BUCCAL:
Buccal is simply a term that refers to an item that would dissolver under the tongue. Some steroids allegedly dissolve under the tongue and are absorbed directly into the blood stream, avoiding the liver and stomach. Therefore you are obviously not supposed to eat or drink whilst taking buccal medication. Personally I think that buccal methods and preparations are a load of shite, but that's just my opinion.

BULKING CYCLE:
This refers to a combination of steroids used specifically for gaining weight, size and strength. These are typically 6-12 week courses that incorporate high anabolic and high androgenic steroids. You would normally see the associated water retention with a bulking cycle.

CATABOLIC:
Also see anti-catabolic. Catabolic is merely the opposite of anabolic. Anabolic refers to a state of growth, catabolic refers to a state of decline.

CYCLE:
This is a phrase used to loosely generalise about the duration of your stack and what drugs you are using. For example, a cutting cycle would define your drug, eating and training style as opposed to a bulking cycle.

CUTTING CYCLE:
See cycle and bulking cycle. A cutting cycle refers to a low calorie, dieting period combined with lower androgen steroids and usually the addition of some kind of aerobic exercises. This is a cycle associated with fat loss, hardening of the muscles and water loss, drying out, to show cuts and muscular definition.

DART:
The use of the word dart is simply another term for a needle. It may not always be appropriate to refer to the direct terminology associated with steroid use. For example instead of saying to your buddy 'you got any steroids, needles and syringes?' it would be more discreet to say 'do you have any gear and darts?'. Thus avoiding potentially difficult situation, were someone not associated with the steroid scene to overhear.

ENDOGENOUS:
This word is a simple reference to an process that occurs naturally in the body, for example estrogen is endogenous in the female body, like wise testosterone is endogenous in the male body (naturally occurring).

ESTROGEN:
Everything that makes a woman a woman, fat deposits on the hips and bum, girly emotions, crying, feminisation of every kind, yup estrogen is responsible. Women naturally produce large amounts of estrogen and tiny amounts of testosterone, as opposed to men who produce large amounts of testosterone and tiny amounts of estrogen.

EXOGENOUS:
The word exogenous refers to the introduction of a chemical or hormone into the body from an external source. Example, steroids would be a exogenous introduction of testosterone to the body. This is the opposite of endogenous (naturally occurring in the body).

GYNOCOMASTIA:
This is covered in the side effects section, but to briefly re-cap, high androgen steroids can convert to estrogen, this will then cause fatty deposits to build up in the pectoral/nipple area. This has varying degrees of severity, varying from a tiny bump and sore nipple to the more obvious 'boy boobs' and 'bitch tits'. Nolvadex keeps the estrogens down to avoid this condition.

METABOLISM:
The thyroid gland controls the body's metabolism level. Your metabolism may be fast, slow or normal, if fast or slow it can be controlled with the use of thyroid drugs such as thyroxin. Usually once this medication has been used for a prolonged period, the thyroid cannot operate without it and the medication is needed for the life span of the user. However, I digress, metabolism is the word used to describe the breakdown and use of food, nutrition and chemicals by the body to produce energy, growth and other bodily functions. If you have a fast metabolism you will be full of nervous energy, constantly burning calories and struggle to gain weight. A slow

metabolism will usually manifest itself in the gain of fat, due to inefficient use of nutrition, reduced energy levels and feelings of apathy and sluggishness.

PIN:
See dart also, another slang term for a needle.

PLATEAU:
This means when the body's levels of growth stop. For example, if you have been on an 8-week bulking cycle sooner or later your gain in body weight will plateau. The same applies for strength and size. At re-occurring points in your body building life span you will go through growth, strength and size increases, at the end of each increase you plateau (the progression halts). An adjustment in nutrition, training style and/or drug use can help break through the plateau and continue on to the next phase of progression.

POINTS:
Yup, you guessed it, another term for pins, darts and needles.

ROID RAGE:
OK, roid rage, it does exist but usually not for a good reason. The intelligent use of a moderate steroid cycle should not present any problems in the average individual, but what's average? Predominantly roid rage will manifest itself in people that are using high dosages of highly anabolic and highly androgenic steroids over prolonged periods. Also anyone who is either mentally unstable, naturally aggressive, has control problems and is in any kind of stressful situation (work, marriage, money, alcohol, dieting etc) will suffer, to a varying degree. My advice is this, don't cop an attitude just cos your getting bigger, there are enough 'aggro idiots' and bullies in this world without any more 'I'm 18 stone and psyched on steroids' freaks making it worse…..chill out. Make sure your life and mind set are as calm and stable as possible before using

steroids, it'll work out better that way. (OK, lecture over, back to the terminology) Roid rage means a nutter who loses his temper and freaks out, then blames it on steroids instead of his own stupidity. (OK, OK, I'm getting off my high horse, I've not been without my own minor outbursts)

SHOTGUN:
No, not a reference to the use of a firearm, but a phrase used to describe the irresponsible steroid user that can't quite manage to absorb any useful information on how to actually eat, train and use drugs properly. Therefore the shotgun method is used, basically the take absolutely everything they can lay their hands on in the hope that something will work. Different to a stack or array, these would refer to an intelligent use of a planned stack in order to achieve a defined goal. Shot gunning is an irresponsible 'free for all' method of trying to achieve the same thing.

STACK:
A stack, is as it suggests, is stacking (using) two or more items that will work in synergy together. Cutting stacks, bulking stacks, long-term stacks etc, basically just the use of multiple items in a strategic and planned manner. See also shotgun and array.

STAGGER:
Yes, too much to drink and then stagger. In the steroid context however it would refer to the use of 2 or more steroid preparations in a specific way. A number of weeks on the first item, as you reach plateau (or preferably before) you would switch to another item, The 2 can overlap by a week or so, or switch completely. See the 3-week blitz example in the cycle section.

SUBCUTANEOUS:
This is sometimes abbreviated to sub-q. A reference to a type

of injection, predominantly using insulin needles, to inject between the skin and muscle. HCG, insulin, Vit B-12 and growth hormone are all water based and these are really the only items that should be injected subcutaneously. All other steroids and associated preparations would be taken orally or injected intramuscularly (into the muscle). No items associated with bodybuilding are made for intravenous use (into the veins).

TESTOSTERONE:

See also estrogen. This is the little beauty!! Testosterone is everything that makes a man a man. It is responsible for muscle growth, deepening off the voice, hair growth, probably anger and violence, low body fat levels and generally everything that separates a man from a woman. Testosterone is the predominant male hormone, although all men produce tiny amounts of the female hormone estrogen, and vice versa.

VIRILIZATION:

Virilization is the manifestation of male characteristics, such as deep voice, hair growth and skin changes in women. Basically if a woman takes the male hormone testosterone she's going to get man like! The types of steroid used, the amounts used and the individual's sensitivity to the preparation will dictate the severity of this. I've never been a huge fan of women bodybuilders, there's no reason that they shouldn't do it or enjoy it, it's just not my bag as it were. A woman that looks butch, hairy and talks with a gravely voice is never going to look good to me. Likewise a bloke that's pumped full of estrogen, develops tits, fat hips and arse and then starts wearing wigs and lipstick aren't going to look to appealing to most women. But that's just my opinion, for what it's worth, horses for courses.

Closing Statement

This is really just a short couple of paragraphs, to reiterate some of the points I made at the beginning of the book. Steroids are NOT the be all and end all of bodybuilding. They are simply a tool that can be used in synergy with a variety of other tools, such as nutrition, training and rest.

I would also recommend that you take the same steps with your training, rest and nutrition as you have done with your quest for knowledge on steroids. Purchase some books on the subjects, then observe, digest and implement the information provided in a sensible manner.

There is no myth or magic with steroids, neither is there an illusive or magic pill that will make you a granite giant. The quest for growth is a culmination of genetics, scientific information and application of consistent techniques. A numbskull that eats everything, takes every drug and throws around the heaviest weights he can find will surely grow in some shape or form. However the fine carving of a powerful and structured quality physique is not a task that is a result of ignorance or chance. Learn your trade and apply your knowledge in a methodical and structured manner. This way most of the chances, mistakes, mishap's and injuries can be reduced if not completely avoided and growth will occur in a more defined and positive manner.

This book has not been written as a 'how to' manual or as a suggestion to what you should or shouldn't do. I am not a doctor or an advisor, I have no qualifications in the field of biochemistry. I merely offer the information that I have learned over the years. This information has been gleaned from a wide variety of sources over a number over years, more than a decade. It is a culmination of knowledge absorbed from text books, medical journals and manuals, conversations with pro bodybuilders, top contenders of the sport, and of course personal application and use of many of the stacks, techniques and drugs that I describe. To that end this book is merely a porthole to that information for your reference. Thank you.

Notes

Notes

Notes